The First Transcontinental Air Service

The Story of the Tin Goose and the Iron Horse

The First Transcontinental Air Service

The Story of the Tin Goose and the Iron Horse

by Richard L. Taylor

Franklin Watts
New York / Chicago / London / Toronto / Sydney
A First Book

This book is dedicated to my grandson,
Maxwell Robert Taylor,
who will experience aviation wonders
of which I can only dream

Library of Congress Cataloging-in-Publication Data

Taylor, Richard L.
The first transcontinental air service: the story of the Tin Goose and
the iron horse / Richard L. Taylor
p.   cm. — (A First book)
Includes bibliographical references and index.
ISBN 0-531-20186-4
1. Aeronautics, Commercial—United States—History—Juvenile literature.
2. Aeronautics and states—United States—History—Juvenile literature.
[1. Aeronautics, Commercial.] I. Title. II. Series.
HE9803.A3T38 1995
387.7'0973—dc20   94-29073   CIP
                                                   AC

Contents

Foreword

New Year's Day 1914, St. Petersburg, Florida. Pilot Tony Janus opened the throttle of his Benoist flying boat and lifted from the waters of Tampa Bay. Twenty minutes and 22 miles (35 km) later he landed in downtown Tampa, completing the first flight of the world's first scheduled airline.

The St. Petersburg–Tampa Airboat Line stayed in business only a few months, but it was a pioneering venture and a sign of things to come. Only eighteen years later, travelers could fly across the country in twenty-four hours—a giant step from flying across Tampa Bay in twenty minutes.

But some smaller steps had to be taken first. This is the story of one of those steps, an effort to provide the fastest possible travel from coast to coast. It's a story of U.S. airlines and railroads, and how they were combined in 1929 to provide the country's first transcontinental air service.

An ad for the St. Petersburg–Tampa Airboat Line

To understand how these two remarkably different kinds of transportation worked together, the story must begin with a short history of each.

Railroads Everywhere

America's railroad system began formally on Christmas Day in 1830, when a steam-powered locomotive named *The Best Friend of Charleston* pulled five cars along a track near Charleston, South Carolina. It was only a 6-mile (10-km) ride for the 141 passengers, but it was the first scheduled steam railroad passenger service in the United States.

The Best Friend was followed by larger, more powerful locomotives, and the steam engine on wheels—known popularly as the "iron horse"—soon took over from the canalboats and animal-drawn wagons that were the conventional ways of moving people and goods.

Although paved roads connected some of the larger cities, most of these early highways had only two lanes, and the farther west a traveler went, the worse the roads became. On the other hand, railways developed because the steam engine was a far more efficient means of moving cargo than were horses. While construction of a horse or coach trail was easier than laying the tracks for a railroad, massive federal government land grants encouraged the development of railways. A network of tracks soon spread over most of the country. By the end of the Civil War most towns in the eastern part of the United States were served by the railroads, and just about everything that needed to be transported from one place to another went by train.

In 1869, tracks of the Union Pacific Railroad (building westward) and the Central Pacific Railroad (building toward the east) met at Promontory Point, Utah. Now there was a system of railroads that connected the east and west coasts of the United States. The first transcontinental railroad was a reality.

The Best Friend of Charleston

Winter weather was often a problem for train travel. Sometimes trains were nearly covered over by sudden snow-storms or blizzards (left).

From the time of the completion of the transcontinental railroad until the arrival of the airplane, rail travel was the fastest way to travel across the United States. Locomotives with the power of thousands of horses pulled long trains at speeds that no other mode of transportation at the time could match. Trains were sometimes stopped by breakdowns or bad weather, but it didn't happen very often. And when the sun went down, trains didn't have to stop. They just kept going, clicking off mile after mile all night long, stopping only to take on coal and water.

By the late 1920s, improved engines and roadbeds made it possible to get from one coast to the other by train in seventy-two hours—even though many passengers had to sit in a straight-backed "day coach" seat for three days and nights. Most trains

Passenger train service was often simple and spare. These straight-backed seats were "home" to travelers for as many as three days.

With the invention of the Pullman sleeper car, overnight train travel became much more civilized. The berths were stored overhead above seats during the day and pulled down at night by porters.

While some cars were spartan in their appointments, private cars could be very elegant and include every comfort a traveler might require.

had dining cars and club cars for relaxing, but day-coach passengers had to sleep as best they could in their seats.

For passengers who were more interested in comfort than the cost of the train ticket, the railroads introduced the "Pullman" car, named for its inventor, George Pullman. Pullman cars had larger, more comfortable seats than those in day coaches. And when it was time to go to bed, a porter folded the seats out of the way and replaced them with upper and lower berths that had been stored overhead. Curtains provided privacy for the passengers, who slept soundly while the train raced on through the night. Washrooms were usually provided at the ends of each car.

For those travelers wishing the ultimate in affordable comfort, the compartment car was also available, also often built by the Pullman Company. These cars provided compartments for two to four people, with washroom facilities included in a "roomette."

Unless you owned a private railroad car (and some very wealthy people did), going by Pullman was the finest and fastest way to travel. In 1929, the Pullman would play a major part in the creation of the first transcontinental air service in the United States.

Airplanes, War, and Progress

The First World War ended in 1918, fifteen years after the Wright brothers accomplished the world's first successful powered flight. The war took a terrible toll in human lives and national resources for all the countries involved, but the demands of military aviation resulted in technical progress that might have taken much longer in peacetime.

For example, speed was very important. When the war began, some planes were able to fly more than 100 miles (161 km) per hour, but many airplanes were still flying at slower speeds. By the end of the war, the speed record was 153.9 miles (247 km) per hour.

The ability of airplanes to carry heavy loads was also important. At first, pilots merely leaned out of the cockpits of their tiny single-engine reconnaissance planes and dropped handheld bombs on the enemy. By the end of World War I, both sides had real bombers—big airplanes with several engines that were designed

World War I brought about rapid advance in aviation technology.
(above) This Martin bomber, considered a remarkable plane for 1919,
carried four crew members and five machine guns. (below) During
World War I, planes not only carried the weapons of war but also
transported the wounded to hospitals.

specifically to carry heavy bombs and drop them with a precision not possible before.

During these years, airplane engines came in for their share of attention, too. In 1903, the Wright *Flyer* made the world's first powered flight with a 12-horsepower engine the brothers had built in their own shop. It was hard to start, it would quit after just a few minutes because it had no lubrication, and it shook so hard it loosened the airplane's wires and braces.

There was not much improvement in the first few years after the Wright brothers' flight. Airplane

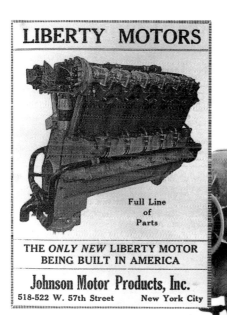

Newly improved and more powerful engines also helped advance early aviation technology.

engines were made by hand one at a time, and each one was a little bit different from the others. As a result, airplane engines were not very reliable. Early pilots gained much experience in making emergency landings, mainly because their engines quit frequently during flight.

The needs of the military forced manufacturers to design better engines, and by the end of World War I, the newer engines were much more reliable. By 1929, powerful *and* reliable airplane engines were available and would become very important to the United States' first transcontinental air service.

Aviation Begins to Grow Up

Americans began to realize the importance of airplanes in the years following World War I. Some of those most interested in aviation were pilots who bought war-surplus airplanes and became "barnstormers." There were no rules in this new business, and barnstormers flew their rickety planes from one town to the next, landing in cow pastures and cornfields, putting on air shows and taking people for joyrides. These pioneering aviators introduced thousands of Americans to the wonder of flight.

But some of the United States' early pilots didn't want the difficult lifestyle of the barnstormers. They preferred to stay at home, working from their own airfields, offering flight instruction, sightseeing rides, and airplane repairs. They tried to sell transportation by air, but the traveling public wasn't quite ready to give up on the old-reliable railroads. Nor were the existing aircraft able to equal the railroads in comfort and reli-

Air shows, complete with daring feats such as wing walking, were quite popular during the early part of the twentieth century.

ability. Nevertheless, the barnstormers and the stay-at-home aviators planted the seeds that grew into America's airlines.

The U.S. federal government played as big a part in airline development as it had in that of the railroads. In 1925, the U.S. Congress passed the Kelly Act, which ended the Army Air Service's job of carrying the mail and opened the business to privately owned companies. Airmail contracts included a subsidy (a guaranteed price) for each pound of mail that was carried. Encouraged by this promise from the government, new airline companies bought airplanes and equipment, and investors put up money to make the airmail business grow.

And grow it did. Small airlines appeared all over the country, many of them staffed with ex-barnstormers who welcomed the opportunity to earn a regular salary as commercial airline pilots. One of these pilots was Charles A. Lindbergh, who would become world famous in 1927 for his solo flight across the Atlantic Ocean. He was hired in 1925 as the chief pilot for Robertson Aircraft Corporation, an airmail carrier based in St. Louis, Missouri.

The early airline entrepreneurs weren't much interested in carrying passengers. They were paid according

Because of the vast distances between cities on the east and west coasts of the United States, the post office has always sought quicker methods to deliver the mail. Scheduled air service and the development of new airlines were a direct result of this need.

to the amount of mail they could pack into their air-planes. Most of the airplanes were hand-me-downs from the military and were never intended to carry passengers. But now and then, there would be room for a hardy soul who needed to get somewhere in a hurry.

A trip in one of these flying mail trucks was uncomfortable, noisy, and hot or cold depending on the time of year. Passengers were often seated in an open cockpit on a pile of mail sacks. Sometimes the pilot would throw another sack onto a rider's lap—every pound of mail meant more money for the company.

Of course there were always the problems of engine

Mail planes provided their passengers with almost nothing. Comforts such as enclosed passenger cabins, food service, and comfortable seats were unavailable.

failures and bad weather. Passengers never knew when their "airliner" might be forced to land in a farmer's field, whereupon they—and the sacks of mail—would continue their journey by train.

Air transportation became more profitable as the volume of airmail increased. With these profits, airline companies bought larger airplanes with better accommodations for passengers. To help continue the growth of this new industry and make flying safer for the traveling public, the Air Commerce Act was enacted by Congress in 1926. Among other things, it provided funds to build emergency airfields and lighting systems for night flying. The act also laid down strict regulations for building airplanes and licensing pilots.

When the Air Commerce Act was passed, there were only nineteen airlines doing business in the United States. But the number grew rapidly, and America soon led the world in air transportation. In 1929, the airline companies flew more than 90,000 miles (144,841 km) every day.

America's airlines were alive and well, but a traveler still couldn't buy an airline ticket for a trip across the country.

Trains and Planes Join Forces

Clement M. Keys learned about business during the years he spent as a newspaper reporter in New York City's financial district. He left the newspaper business in the early 1920s and put together his own financial empire. When he recognized the tremendous future of air transportation, he began to build an aviation empire.

In 1928, the airplanes that carried the mail from San Francisco to Chicago also carried two passengers. Upon landing in Chicago, the mail was transferred to another airline for the flight to New York, but the passengers

Clement M. Keys

The federal Air Commerce Act required lighted airways, which helped facilitate the development of passenger air service in the late 1920s.

had to continue by train. The Chicago–New York airline had no interest in carrying passengers.

Clement Keys was aware of this and decided that his aviation empire should include a way to get air travelers from one coast to the other in the shortest possible time. That meant flying at night, something that wasn't part of air travel in 1928. Some of the lighted airways funded by the Air Commerce Act had been completed, but night flying wasn't considered safe enough yet for passenger flights. This was especially true over the mountains—the Rockies and the Sierras in the West, the Alleghenies in the East.

So Clement Keys came up with an idea that would solve the problem. He knew that an all-air trip from coast to coast would require three or four days because the airplanes had to stop at night. He also knew that the fastest trains needed seventy-two hours to get from one coast to the other. Why not combine the two—air travel during the day, train travel during the night— and provide forty-eight-hour service from coast to coast?

Why not indeed? Keys formed a new company called Transcontinental Air Transport, or TAT. The new airline would eliminate the inconvenience of changing railroads and buying several tickets to complete the trip. With TAT, it would be one ticket and one airline from coast to coast.

Keys took his plans to General W. W. Atterbury, president of the Pennsylvania Railroad, and found an enthusiastic partner in the new venture. "We are no longer railroads alone," said the general, "we are transportation companies. We must be prepared to offer railroad service where it is most desirable, or bus service, or service by airplane."

That solved the problem of getting passengers over

the Allegheny Mountains at night. The Atchison, Topeka, and Santa Fe Railroad agreed to handle the ground transportation on the western segment of the route, and Keys turned his attention to choosing the proper airplane for his new company.

Pennsylvania Station in New York City was the home of the rail partner in TAT's planned rail–air service across North America.

The Tin Goose

Lots of airplanes have nicknames. For example, there was a military cargo plane that vibrated so much in flight it became known as "Old Shaky." One of the early, underpowered jet fighters needed a very long runway for takeoff, and it was called the "Lead Sled." The DC-3 will always be known as the "Gooney Bird" to those who flew it.

And so it was with the Ford trimotor, the most successful of the early all-metal passenger airplanes. Someone nicknamed it the "Tin Goose," maybe because it was built by Henry Ford, the man who made another "tin" vehicle famous—the Model T automobile, also known as the "Tin Lizzie."

The Tin Goose evolved from earlier airplanes that also used corrugated metal and internal wing bracing. These unique design features were first used in 1915 by the Junkers Aircraft Company in Germany, followed by the Stout Metal Plane Company in the United States.

The Ford trimotor airplane, popularly known as the "Tin Goose"

It looked like Stout's "Air Sedan" could be easily mass-produced, so Henry Ford bought the company and built a factory and an airport. The first Ford trimotor was completed in 1926.

All things considered, the Tin Goose was perhaps America's finest airliner when TAT began its air–rail service. It was not the biggest, and certainly not the fastest, but in terms of reliability, passenger comfort, and load-carrying ability, the Tin Goose was hard to beat. Fords were used by all the major airlines during the 1920s and 1930s, and some of them are still flying today.

The Tin Goose was an economical airplane, mostly because it was lighter than other airplanes of its size. Fully loaded, a TAT trimotor weighed about 11,000 pounds (5,000 kg), but more than a third of that weight was "useful load"—passengers, baggage, and fuel.

One reason for the Tin Goose's light weight was the metal from which it was made. Some of the airplane structure was steel (engine mounts, landing gear, and so on), but the entire outer covering was duralumin. This aluminum alloy is nearly as strong as steel but is much lighter.

The duralumin was corrugated, making the entire surface look something like an accordion with curved pleats. (If a Ford trimotor's wings were rolled flat, they would be nearly as long as the wings of a Boeing 727, a

The duralumin covering of Ford trimotors gave the airplanes quite an unusual textured surface but added to their structural strength.

This assembly-line photo shows the trimotor airplane before the duralumin "skin" has been added.

modern jet airliner.) Corrugation made it possible for the skin to carry some of the structural load, doing away with some of the heavy bracing required by other airplanes.

The wings of the Tin Goose were cantilevered (braced internally) and didn't need the struts and wires that created tremendous amounts of drag on other airplanes. The power that would have been needed to push struts and wires through the air was used to make the airplane more efficient.

The trimotor's wings are highly curved on the upper surface. Here the wing structure is added to the fuselage of a Tin Goose under construction.

The wings were also very thick, with a highly cambered (curved) upper surface, a design that helped produce a great deal of lift at low speeds. The Ford trimotor never won any prizes for speed, but it could take off and land in a very short distance with a full load.

This was a bonus for TAT, because several of its airports were little more than grass fields or cinder strips. No problem for the Tin Goose, which could take off and land at 60 miles (97 km) per hour—about the same as today's training airplanes, which carry only two people and weigh only 1,500 pounds (700 kg).

TAT's Fords were powered by three 425-horsepower, air-cooled radial engines, each with nine cylinders in a starlike arrangement around the crankshaft. Radial engines were used on most large airplanes in the 1920s, mostly because of their light weight and reliability.

The cockpit of a Ford trimotor was an exercise in simplicity. There was a big round control wheel and a set of rudder pedals for each pilot, three throttles, mixture controls, and ignition switches for the engines. The instrument panel contained only the essentials: airspeed indicator, altimeter, turn indicator, clock, and

The instrumentation in the trimotor was kept to a minimum and included only the essentials.

This closeup of the tail section of a trimotor shows how the tail wheel was free to swivel.

instruments for the center engine. Instruments for the other two engines were mounted outside, on the engines themselves.

The Tin Goose's tail wheel was free to swivel, and on the ground the airplane behaved like a giant weather vane, always trying to turn into the wind. Steering was accomplished with asymmetrical power (speeding up one of the outboard engines to pull the airplane around a turn) or differential braking (applying brake pressure to just one of the main wheels). A long metal brake bar rose out of the cockpit floor between the pilot seats. Pulled straight back, it braked both wheels, but moved to the left or right, it braked one wheel at a time.

Henry Ford's early automobiles provided the bare minimum when it came to comfort and convenience, and his early airplanes were no different. The standard Tin Goose had no effective soundproofing, little cabin heat, and plain wicker seats. TAT's airplanes were a bit fancier, with more comfortable seats, pillow headrests, individual reading lights, and a number of luxurious appointments that contributed to the airline's "first class" image.

Ford trimotors established a remarkable safety record during the years they were used by the airlines. This was largely because of the reliable Pratt & Whitney engines. The Tin Goose, like all other multi-engine airplanes of that time, needed all of its engines in order to maintain altitude. Lightly loaded, a Ford might be able to fly level if one engine failed, but on a typical airline trip with passengers and baggage, a *two*-motored trimotor would sink slowly out of the sky.

Designers of the Tin Goose tried to equal or exceed the elegance and comfort of the finer railroad passenger cars.

TAT — "The Lindbergh Line"

Clement Keys wanted nothing but the best when it came to selecting the equipment, facilities, and personnel for Transcontinental Air Transport. There would be no airmail subsidy from the government, so the new airline focused on attracting passengers who were willing to pay more to get from coast to coast in less time than was possible by railroad travel alone. TAT's customers would expect first-class treatment.

In 1928, the year after his pioneering solo transatlantic flight, Col. Charles A. Lindbergh was the most famous aviator in the world and had become very active in promoting air transportation. He accepted a position as TAT's consulting aeronautical engineer and chairman of its technical committee. TAT began to call itself "The Lindbergh Line."

One of Lindbergh's jobs was to determine the airline's route across the country. He had to consider geography, airports, and railroads already in existence, and the most efficient locations for the air–rail transfer points.

After careful study and many survey flights, Lindbergh set up an air route that went generally southwest from Columbus, Ohio (the first transfer point), to Waynoka, Oklahoma. The Santa Fe Railroad then carried TAT passengers overnight from Waynoka

Executives of TAT included Charles A. Lindbergh (second from right) and Clement Keys (far right)

to Clovis, New Mexico (the second transfer point). When air travel resumed the next morning, the trimotors flew almost due west across the mountains to Los Angeles. Eastbound passengers would retrace the route in the opposite direction.

Col. Lindbergh decided upon eleven airfields for the transcontinental service, most of them existing airports. TAT had to build its own airports and passenger terminals at three of the western stops: Waynoka, Oklahoma; Clovis, New Mexico; and Kingman, Arizona. All totaled, TAT spent more than $1.5 million on ground facilities—in today's dollars, that would be more than $45 million.

One of the remote offices of the private meteorological system that TAT established to provide the latest weather information to its pilots.

Weather was a considerable concern because the Tin Goose was not equipped to fly in the clouds—"on instruments." Because of this, TAT pilots needed frequent, accurate reports to help them avoid areas of bad weather. An advertisement for the new coast-to-coast service explained how this problem was solved:

WATCHERS AT 82 DIFFERENT POINTS GUARD
THESE SWIFT PLANES

A private meteorological system—designed to be the inspiration of airlines of the future—has been worked out in conjunction with governmental and other agencies. Also an elaborate system of communications (telephone, radiophone, wireless)—making it possible for planes in flight to receive weather reports compiled from observations at 82 different points along the route.

As the date for the inaugural flights approached, TAT began to let people know about the new service. Advertisements in newspapers and magazines used a basic theme—"Coast to Coast in 48 hours"—and such phrases as:

"By night a luxurious train—by day a safe, swift plane!"

". . . airplanes have been most rigorously tested . . ."

". . . the highest standards of efficiency, speed, safety . . ."

". . . emergency landing fields have been laid out at regular intervals along the carefully prepared routes . . ."

"Soar like the eagle! Swift and sure, these planes glide smoothly over some of the most beautiful scenery in America."

". . . your flight is direct—with just enough stops to provide variety . . ."

There was also a twenty-minute promotional film titled *Coast to Coast in 48 Hours*. Col. Lindbergh and the Tin Goose were the stars of the film, which emphasized the speed and luxury of the TAT air–rail combination.

There were test flights, of course—dress rehearsals to make certain that no detail had been overlooked. Company officials had promised that they would begin service "when everything is ready—not one minute before!" In July 1929 all the preparations were complete, and TAT was ready to begin the first transcontinental air service.

Coast to Coast in 48 Hours

When the first train left New York and the first airplane left Los Angeles, most of the passengers were TAT officials, newspaper reporters, and special guests. But there may have been one make-believe traveler who kept a make-believe diary of the journey from coast to coast. It began in New York City on that historic evening in July 1929.

Sunday, July 7, on board the *Airway Limited*

Arrived at Pennsylvania Station in New York City about four o'clock this afternoon. A crowd of reporters, photographers, and spectators, especially around the Ford trimotor (a real, full-size airplane!) on display in the middle of the station. I wonder how they got it in here? I can hardly wait to fly on the Tin Goose tomorrow.

We left New York at exactly 6:05 P.M., right on schedule. The train is named the *Airway Limited* in honor of the first air–rail service across the country.

The famed aviatrix Amelia Earhart (directly behind the ribbon and next to C. M. Keys) helped inaugurate TAT's rail–air service from Penn Station in New York City on July 7, 1929.

Had a fine meal in the dining car, then chatted with other passengers. It's now ten o'clock and the porter has just made up my Pullman berth. I want to get a good night's sleep—tomorrow will be a long day.

Monday, July 8, Columbus, Ohio

Arrived here at 7:35 A.M. Three thousand people standing in the rain to watch the first train-plane connection from N.Y. to L.A. Two trimotors (one is named the *City of Columbus*) will carry nineteen passengers westbound.

The *Airway Limited* stopped right beside the passenger terminal at Port Columbus (a good name for an airport!). I understand Col. Lindbergh chose the terminal's location next to the tracks.

Railway stations were constructed to connect the train service to the air service. This photo shows construction of the link at Columbus, Ohio.

It's now eight o'clock, and they're calling us to board the Tin Goose—the reports show better weather to the west.

Monday, July 8, aboard the Ford trimotor *City of Columbus*

My first airplane ride! Off the ground as scheduled at 8:15 A.M. In three and a half hours (8:45 A.M. Pacific time) another Ford will leave Los Angeles with the first eastbound passengers.

The Tin Goose is noisier than expected. Not much conversation among passengers because we have to shout to be heard, even across the narrow aisle. The steward has given us cotton for earplugs . . . I hope it helps, because there's a full day of flying ahead.

Flying 2,000 feet (635 m) above the ground. The steward has given each passenger a map to follow the flight . . . it's easy to pick out the cities and towns as we fly overhead.

Next stop, Indianapolis, Indiana. At 110 miles (177 km) per hour, we should land there at 9:13 A.M. Central time.

Monday, July 8, Indianapolis, Indiana

Landed here on schedule. A fifteen-minute rest stop while the Tin Goose was refueled, then off again for St. Louis, Missouri, two hours and thirty-five minutes away. That trip would take almost a full day by car!

The *City of Columbus* photographed in flight

Monday, July 8, Waynoka, Oklahoma

Got so interested in watching the world roll by below that I forgot to make entries at St. Louis, Kansas City, and Wichita. Now I have time to catch up.

The steward served hot soup at midmorning, and we

First-class food service, including hot food, silver, and china, was among the many conveniences provided by TAT.

had lunch between St. Louis and Kansas City . . . broiled chicken kept hot in Thermos jugs. Between K.C. and Wichita, we had sandwiches and tea. Everything is "first class," just as an ocean liner . . . china plates, silverware, linen napkins, etc.

The Kansas City airport is very close to the downtown area . . . a big crowd watched the trimotor come in.

TAT's airport at Wichita is huge . . . 640 acres (260 ha) with runways in just about every direction because the trimotors can't handle strong crosswinds on takeoff and landing . . . and the pilot says there's *always* a strong crosswind in Kansas! Landed at Waynoka at about 6:30 P.M. I feel like I've been riding inside a drum for ten hours. The Tin Goose's corrugated metal sides seem to amplify the engine noise. I wonder if my ears will ever stop ringing!

It was raining when we got off the plane in Waynoka, but we stayed dry, thanks to the canopy-covered walkways (they're at all TAT terminals) from airplane to terminal. Rode from airport to the Harvey House restaurant in an Aerocar, specially designed for TAT. It's a fancy, three-wheeled trailer—a living room on wheels—pulled by a Studebaker coupe.

Covered walkways, such as this one in Columbus, Ohio, were standard at all eleven airports that TAT flew into.

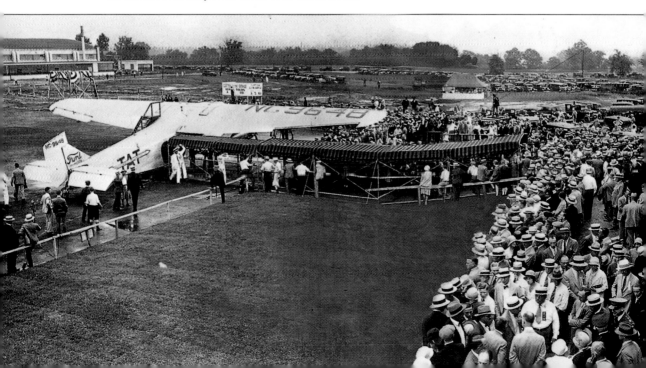

There's an Aerocar at every terminal . . . nothing but the best for TAT passengers!

I'm writing this from my Pullman berth aboard the *Missionary*, the Santa Fe train that departed Waynoka at 11:00 P.M. We'll arrive in Clovis, New Mexico, at 8:20 tomorrow morning . . . believe me, I'm ready for bed!

TAT's passengers paid a premium for transcontinental rail–air service. In return, convenience and comfort were provided at every point. The Aerocar was developed to transport travelers from airports to rail stations.

Tuesday, July 9, Clovis, New Mexico

Aerocar took us from train station to airport with a quick stop for breakfast on the way. Back in the air at 9:10 A.M. (they really run this railroad on *time!*), bound for Albuquerque, New Mexico, about two hours to the west.

Yesterday, noticed that cities and towns were much farther apart as we flew across Kansas, Oklahoma, and the Texas panhandle. We're over the southwest desert now—nothing but sand, dried up streams, and an occasional small town.

The terrain is also getting higher . . . we'll have to climb to 8,000 feet (2,438 m) to clear the mountains just east of Albuquerque.

Arrived in Albuquerque a few minutes after ten o'clock, Mountain Time. Another time zone crossed . . . one more to go!

The Albuquerque airport lies 5,352 feet (1,631 m) above sea level . . . the highest airport on the TAT system. Our Tin Goose needed a lot more runway for takeoff because of the thinner air at this altitude, made worse by the midday heat . . . 105°F (40°C) in the shade!

The heat also helps create bumpy air, and several passengers have gotten sick. Unpleasant for the rest of us in a small cabin like this, but I guess it can't be helped . . . motion sickness is part of traveling by air. The *City of Columbus* was the first TAT airplane to land at Albuquerque . . . the eastbound flight from L.A. was delayed yesterday because of bad weather. We've made history!

Tuesday, July 9, Kingman, Arizona

Hot, bumpy, uncomfortable two-hour trip from Albuquerque to Winslow, Arizona. Flew at 9,000 feet (2,743 m) above sea level to clear the mountains, which continue as far as I can see in all directions.

Winslow became famous yesterday. Col. Charles Lindbergh was at the controls when the first eastbound TAT flight landed in midafternoon. Lindbergh stayed in Winslow overnight, then—to our delight!—climbed into the pilot's seat and flew us to Los Angeles.

Uneventful flight from Winslow to Kingman. The Grand Canyon was off to our right, but too far away to see.

Another fifteen-minute stop in Kingman . . . we stretch our legs, the Tin Goose is refueled, and we're off on the last leg of the trip.

California, here we come!!

Tuesday, July 9, Los Angeles, California

Crossed the Colorado River 35 miles (56 km) from

River, near Swanee, New Mexico, shown in the upper left. (center) The famous Meteor Crater, almost a mile across, formed centuries ago by a heavenly projectile which buried itself hundreds of feet in the ground. Lower left, is the awe inspiring Grand Canyon, with the threadlike Colorado River in its depths.

The views from the Tin Goose were spectacular: (upper left) the San Jose River near Swanee, New Mexico; (center) a TAT plane over Meteor Crater; and (lower right) a view of the Grand Canyon

Kingman, flew across the southern tip of Nevada, and then . . . into California at last!

At 5 P.M. Pacific Time, the *City of Columbus* rolled to a stop in front of the Grand Central Air Terminal in Glendale, 10 miles (16 km) north of downtown Los Angeles. The first transcontinental air service was in the history books, and I was part of it!

The passengers on TAT's first westward-bound flight are met by
a grandstand of spectators in Los Angeles. The Aerocar carried
passengers into the city.

Afterword

From the very beginning, TAT tried to make its air service as luxurious and convenient as possible. During the first several months, the novelty of this new way to travel from coast to coast attracted enough passengers to require a two-airplane schedule in each direction every day.

But the fine meals, the Aerocars, the personal radio communications (forerunner of today's airborne telephones), and all the other extras weren't enough to offset the high cost of an airline ticket from coast to coast. On top of that, the first winter's bad weather caused so many cancellations that "TAT" became known as "Take a Train."

Even at reduced prices, ticket sales declined, and after a year of operation the ten-seat trimotors seldom carried more than two or three paying passengers. The airline's financial situation grew steadily worse; it was the beginning of the end for TAT.

In the mid-1930s, the second rail segment was abandoned in favor of an overnight stop in Tulsa, Oklahoma. The trip was shortened to thirty-six hours when TAT planes were able to fly from New York or Los Angeles to Kansas City, remain there overnight, and continue the next morning.

Clement Keys' air–rail combination was an expensive experiment, and it became obsolete in a very short period of time because of rapid advances in air transportation. As more of the nation's airways were equipped with signal lights to guide pilots, night flying became practical. By 1932, airline travel from coast to coast had been reduced to twenty-four hours.

TAT had lost $2.7 million in eighteen months and was nearly bankrupt. Late in 1930, the company merged with Western Air Express. The new corporation, Transcontinental and Western Air, Inc., eventually became Trans World Airlines.

TAT's Ford trimotors can hardly be compared to today's 500-mile-per-hour (805-km) jet airliners, but the Tin Goose pioneered the transcontinental flights we now take for granted. Today, a nonstop flight from New York to Los Angeles takes about six hours, in air-conditioned, pressurized comfort 7 or 8 miles (11 or 13 km) above the earth.

If you should ever get the opportunity to fly an airliner from coast to coast, think of the Ford trimotor and its uncomfortable passengers, plodding along at 110 miles (177 km) per hour. And remember that it all began with Clement Keys' plan to speed travelers "From Coast to Coast in 48 Hours."

Facts, Figures, Important Dates

The Ford trimotor—The "Tin Goose"

The Ford Motor Company built 199 trimotors between 1926 and 1932. There were several models produced, each one a bit larger, more powerful, or capable of carrying larger loads than the last.

These specifications are representative of the Model 5-AT, used by Transcontinental Air Transport in its air–rail service:

Ford Model 5-AT-A
Span — 77 feet 10 inches (24 m)
Length — 49 feet 10 inches (15 m)
Height — 13 feet 8 inches (4 m)
Empty weight — 6,700 pounds (3,040 kg)
Useful load — 4,100 pounds (1,860 kg)
Maximum weight — 10,800 pounds (4,900 kg)
Maximum speed — 130 mph (208 km)
Cruising speed — 110 mph (177 km)
Landing speed — 59 mph (95 km)

Power — Three Pratt & Whitney Wasp radial
    engines. These nine-cylinder, air-cooled engines
    produced 425 horsepower each.
Passenger capacity — 10

The TAT Journey from Coast to Coast

Air miles — 2,343 (3,700 km)

Rail miles — 970 (1,561 km)

Total fare — $337 to $403, depending on the passenger's
    choice of railroad accommodations. (These fares would
    be roughly $10,000 to $12,000 in 1990s dollars.)

Baggage allowance — 30 pounds (14 kg) per passenger

Total time coast-to-coast — Westbound, 49 hours,
    49 minutes. Eastbound, 46 hours, 5 minutes
    (The eastbound trip was faster because of prevailing
    westerly winds.)

Shortest scheduled air segment — 1 hour; from Waynoka,
    Oklahoma, to Wichita, Kansas (eastbound)

Longest scheduled air segment — 2 hours, 48 minutes;
    from Kingman, Arizona, to Los Angeles (westbound)

Air-rail Transfer Points — Columbus, Ohio; Waynoka,
    Oklahoma; Clovis, New Mexico

Service began — from New York, July 7, 1929; from
    Los Angeles, July 8, 1929

Service ended — October 1930

For Further Reading

Boyne, Walter J. *The Smithsonian Book of Flight for Young People.* New York: Atheneum, 1988.

Everds, John. *It Began with Jenny: A History of Air Transportation.* Northbrook, Ill.: Hubbard Press, 1972.

Kerrod Robin. *Air,* vol. 2 of *The Silver Burdett Encyclopedia of Transport.* Morristown, N.J.: Silver Burdett, 1983.

Spangenburg, Ray, and Diane Moser. *The Story of Air Transport in America.* New York: Facts on File, 1992.

The Visual Dictionary of Flight. New York: Dorling Kindersley, 1992.

Index

About the Author

Richard L. Taylor is an associate professor emeritus in the Department of Aviation at Ohio State University, having retired in 1988 after twenty-two years as an aviation educator. At retirement, he was the Director of Flight Operations and Training, with responsibility for all flight training and university air transportation. He holds two degrees from Ohio State University: a B.S. in agriculture and an M.A. in journalism.

His first aviation book, *Instrument Flying*, was published in 1972, and continues in its third edition as one of the best-sellers in popular aviation literature. Since then, he has written five more books for pilots, and hundreds of articles and columns for aviation magazines.

Taylor began his aviation career in 1955 when he entered U.S. Air Force pilot training, and after four years on active duty continued his military activity as a reservist until retirement as a major and command pilot in 1979.

Still active as a pilot and accident investigator, as well as a writer, Taylor flies frequently for business and pleasure. His books for Franklin Watts include *First Flight*, *The First Solo Flight Around the World*, *The First Flight Across the United States*, and *The First Supersonic Flight*, *The First Human-Powered Flight*, and *The First Transcontinental Air Service*. He and his wife, Nancy, live in Dublin, a suburb of Columbus, Ohio.